GW00786742

LITTLE BOOK OF
BLONDES

'What's great about going
blonde is that with so little you can
change yourself so much.'
ORLANDO PITA, HAIR STYLIST

'Not all that tempts your wand'ring eyes
And heedless hearts, is lawful prize;
Nor all, that glisters, gold.'
THOMAS GRAY 1716–1771

THE
LITTLE BOOK OF
BLONDES

Angela Lox

Michael O'Mara Humour

First published in Great Britain in 2000 by
Michael O'Mara Books Limited
9 Lion Yard, Tremadoc Road
London SW4 7NQ

A CIP catalogue record for this book is available
from the British Library

ISBN 1-85479-558-9

1 3 5 7 9 10 8 6 4 2

Edited by David Brown
Designed and typeset by K DESIGN
Printed in China by Leo Paper Products Ltd

Angela would like to thank
David Brown for his help
and advice in the writing of this
book and, most of all, would
like to thank him for taking
her seriously and for not
asking if the book, unlike
her hair, is all her own work.

'Maybe it's the hair. Maybe it's the teeth. Maybe it's the intellect. No, it's the hair.'

TOM SHALES ON FARRAH FAWCETT

'Gentlemen always seem to remember blondes.'

ANITA LOOS, *Gentlemen Prefer Blondes*

Introduction . . .

So what is it with blondes? On the one
hand seven out of ten men will turn
round in the street to look at a passing
blonde woman. On the other, most
people assume that blondes are stupid.

Many are disdainful of those who
depend on beauty products to enhance
their attractiveness to others. Are there
not better ways? Brainpower, for
example? Possibly, but statistics show
that a splash of peroxide is a quick and
sure way to get you noticed.

Such prejudices are a little unfair on natural blondes, of course, who are not necessarily out to impress, but who, through no fault of their own, most probably have to endure a lifetime of such comments as, 'I can see that hair colour comes right out of your head,' or 'I guess you need to use mascara,' – to say nothing of 'matching collars and cuffs'.

To shed more light on the subject of blondes and blonds, I have put together this engaging medley of quotations, historical facts and social insights.

I have tried to be as objective and impartial as possible, but to all those brunettes and redheads out there I say, let us not be too hard on blondes. For some of them do have more colourful lives; we must concede that some gentlemen do prefer them; and remember, it's not nice to be cruel to dumb animals.

Angela Lox, March 2000

'Her hair that lay along her back
Was yellow like ripe corn.'

DANTE GABRIEL ROSSETTI,
'The Blessed Damozel'

In the Company of Blondes . . .

Let us start by looking at who out there is or was a famous blond/e – from the platinum to the mousy . . .

'So we think of Marilyn who was every man's love affair with America, Marilyn Monroe who was blonde and beautiful and had a sweet little rinky-dink of a voice and all the cleanliness of all the clean American backyards.'

NORMAN MAILER, *Marilyn*

Heading for Stardom –
Hollywood Blond/es . . .

Doris Day, Brad Pitt, Goldie Hawn,
Grace Kelly, Leonardo DiCaprio,
Robert Redford, Gwyneth Paltrow,
Diana Dors, Brigitte Bardot, Michael
Caine, Bette Davis, Daryl Hannah, Drew
Barrymore, Rutger Hauer, Sarah Jessica
Parker, Kenneth Branagh, Emma
Thompson, Pamela Anderson, Rosanna
Arquette, Mae West, Kim Novak, Meryl
Streep, Julie Christie, Tippi Hedren, Peter
O'Toole, Alicia Silverstone,
Carroll Baker, Angie Dickinson,

Veronica Lake, Olivia Newton-John,
Matt Damon, Hayley Mills,
Nicolas Cage, Michelle Pfeiffer,
Meg Ryan, Elisabeth Shue,
Imogen Stubbs, Cate Blanchett,
Ellen Barkin, Lana Turner, Sharon Stone,
Steve McQueen, Jessica Lange,
Greta Garbo, Bo Derek, Betty Grable,
Jane Fonda, Shirley Temple, Cameron Diaz,
Cybill Shepherd, Uma Thurman, Alan Ladd,
Carol Lombard, Julie Andrews,
Macauley Culkin, Woody Harrelson,
Rebecca DeMornay, Candice Bergen,
Catherine Deneuve, Sharon Tate,
Capucine, Heather Graham.

Locks on the Box –
TV Blond/es . . .

Denise Van Outen, Barbara Windsor,
Zoë Ball, Anneka Rice, Anthea Turner,
Pauline Calf, Gaby Roslin, Kirsty Young,
Samantha Janus, Lily Savage, Sara Crowe,
David Soul, Cheryl Ladd, Michelle Collins,
Ulrike Jonsson, Calista Flockhart, Lisa
Kudrow, David Hyde Pierce, Gloria
Hunniford, Helen Mirren, Tori Spelling,
Judy Finnegan, Ellen DeGeneres, Anne
Heche, Esther Rantzen, Caroline Aherne,
Bart Simpson, Paula Yates, Miss Piggy,
Joanna Lumley, Flat Eric, Jilly Goolden,

Gordon the Gopher, Mariella Frostrup,
Bet Lynch, Jimmy Saville, Chris Tarrant,
Barney Rubble, Wendy Richard, Paul
Nicholas, Charlene Tilton, Les Dennis,
June Whitfield, Kimberley Davies, Felicity
Kendal, Farrah Fawcett, William Shatner,
Kes (*Star Trek Voyager*), Flash Gordon,
The Milky Bar Kid, John Boy Walton,
Gail Porter, Amanda Holden,
Simon Pegg, The Brady Bunch, Pamela
Stephenson, Ardal O'Hanlon, Connie
Booth, Vanessa Feltz, Terri Dwyer,
Tamzin Outhwaite, Lara Masters, Jenny
McCarthy, Heather Locklear,
Julia Carling, Buffy the Vampire Slayer,
Lisa Faulkner, Jamie Oliver the Naked
Chef, Anthony Worrall-Thompson.

Going Platinum –
Musical Blond/es . . .

Debbie Harry, Billy Idol, Ronan Keating, Emma Bunton, Rod Stewart, Dave Stewart, Nick Berry, Dolly Parton, Madonna, Ozzy Osbourne, Courtney Love, Benny, Bjorn, Agnetha from Abba, Simon Le Bon, Elaine Paige, David Bowie, Christina Aguilera, Alison Moyet, David Sylvian, Kylie & Jason, Bonnie Tyler, Toyah, Cyndi Lauper, Britney Spears, Natalie & Nicole Appleton, Goldie, Liam Gallagher, Luke & Matt Goss, Gary Barlow, Mark Owen, Robert Plant, Limahl, Dollar, Cerys Matthews, Sting, Lesley Garrett, H from Steps, Jon Bon Jovi.

That Winning Streak – Sporting Blond/es . . .

David Beckham, David Gower, Jack Nicklaus, Dennis Rodman, Bjorn Borg, Chris Evert, Hulk Hogan, Martina Navratilova, Steve Redgrave, Paul Gascoigne, Dean Richards, Mika Hakkinen, Jane Torvill & Christopher Dean, Sharron Davies, James Hunt, Greg Norman, Jacques Villeneuve, David Coulthard, Stefan Edberg, Bobby Moore, Bobby Charlton, Arnold Palmer, Peter Schmeichel, Ian Botham, Shane Warne, Michael Schumacher, Anna Kournikova, David Icke, Fanny Blankers-Coen, Alan Shearer, Steffi Graf, Dennis Bergkamp, Jurgen Klinsmann.

Dyeing Young –
Tragic Blond/es . . .

Marilyn Monroe, Jayne Mansfield,
Ruth Ellis, Diana, Princess of Wales,
John Denver, Jean Harlow, Kurt Cobain,
James Dean, Miss Scarlett, Lolo Ferrari.

Golden Spy – Bond's Blond/es . . .

Ursula Andress, Sean Bean, Daniela
Bianchi, Tania Mallett, Molly Peters,
Catherina von Schell, Britt Ekland,
Blanche Ravalec, Cassandra Harris,
Kristina Wayborn, Kim Basinger, Honor
Blackman, Shirley Eaton, Lynn-Holly
Johnson, Tanya Roberts, Fiona Fullerton,
Maryam d'Abo, Cecile Thomsen, Daphne
Deckers, Judi Dench, Carey Lowell,
Robert Shaw.

A Head for Fashion – Designers' Blondes . . .

Caprice, Claudia Schiffer, Patti Boyd,
Jerry Hall, Barbie, Sindy, Twiggy,
Donatella Versace, Paula Hamilton,
Eva Herzigova, Lisa Butcher,
Christie Brinkley, Sophie Dahl,
Rachel Hunter, Vivienne Westwood,
Kristen Zang, Jodie Kidd,
Jemma Kidd, Karen Mulder,
the Timotei Girl,
Nadja Auerman,
Stella McCartney.

Making Headlines –
Tabloid, Broadsheet &
Bookish Blond/es . . .

Samantha Fox, Emma Noble,
Melinda Messenger, Anna Nicole Smith,
Elisabeth Murdoch, Boris Johnson,
Kate Adie, Jilly Cooper, Patricia Cornwell,
Sebastian Faulks, Fay Weldon,
Angela Lox.

American cartoonist Chic Young produced the famous *Blondie* strip in 1930, later syndicated in more than 1,500 newspapers worldwide. Blondie became an icon to the US forces in World War Two. The British Tommies preferred the *Daily Mirror's* Jane, however, a buxom blonde who regularly lost her clothes for the war effort.

It Blond/es

Tamara Beckwith, Meg Mathews,
Patsy Kensit.

Past-It Blond/es

Princess Michael of Kent,
Barbara Cartland, Ivana Trump,
Peter Stringfellow, Mandy Smith,
Amanda de Cadenet, Twinkle.

Good Colourists –
Arty Blond/es

Andy Warhol
David Hockney
Botticelli's Venus.

Power-Haired Blond/es

Michael Heseltine, Hillary Clinton,
Margaret Thatcher, Prince William,
Eva Peron, General 'Stormin Norman'
Schwarzkopf, La Cicciolina,
Reinhard Heydrich,
Manfred, Baron von Richthofen.

*(Did You Know that a statistically
surprising number of British blondes are
reputed to be supporters of the Liberal
Democrat party?)*

Blonde Ever After –
Fairytale Blond/es

Cinderella, Goldilocks,
Rapunzel, Asterix, Tinker Bell,
Disney's Alice in Wonderland,
Christopher Robin,
Winnie-the-Pooh.

Bright Blond/es

This page is intentionally left blank.

Properties of Blonde Hair . . .

Did you know that blondes have
more hair on their heads
than brunettes?

Blondes: 140,000 hairs
Brunettes: 108,000

A Few Things You Should Know About Blondes . . .

Blondes outnumber brunettes on magazine covers by more than four to one. According to a new survey, 67 per cent of men still turn their heads when they see a blonde walking down the street. Nearly all of the famous movie blondes were born brunettes. Marlene Dietrich, Greta Garbo, Marilyn Monroe, Brigitte Bardot and Catherine Deneuve were, or are, dyed blondes. Anita Loos of *Gentlemen Prefer Blondes* fame, was a brunette. Her first autobiography was called: *This Brunette Prefers Work.*

Once Upon a Time . . .
or All's 'Fair'
in Love and Hair

'Once upon a time there lived the daughter of a king. Her hair was finer than gold and marvellously and wondrously blonde, all curly and fell to her feet. She was called Beauty with the Golden Hair.'

MME D'AULNOY, *La Belle aux Cheveux d'Or*

Our feelings about blondeness are probably formed early in childhood. After all, wouldn't our attitudes and memories be completely changed if Goldilocks had been Gingerlocks, if Cinderella had tight black curly hair and Rapunzel's long tresses had been bright purple in the punk style?

In fairy tales the heroines are always golden-haired. Their bad siblings, not to mention the witches and other nasties, are invariably dark-haired. In the tale *Snow White and Rose Red*, it is the blonde Snow White who gets the prince, whilst Rose Red, a brunette, has to make do with the prince's brother.

Literary Blondes . . .

Traditionally the blonde in literature is rather sickeningly pure and good:

'She was the most winning thing that ever brought sunshine into a desolate house – a real beauty in face . . . and yellow curling hair'

description of Catherine Linton,
in **Wuthering Heights**

'. . . such a beautiful girl! With such rich golden hair . . . and such a bright, innocent, trusting face'

description of Ada Clare in **Bleak House**

There are exceptions. The infamous Becky Sharp in *Vanity Fair* is sandy-haired. Rosamond in *Middlemarch*, who has 'hair of infantile fairness, neither flaxen nor yellow', is vain, shallow and avaricious. Her first husband dies young, 'Lydgate's hair never became white', and Rosamond then marries a rich doctor. The heroine of the book is the dark-haired Dorothea Brooke, 'a girl so handsome and with such prospects'.

The Blonde in History . . .
The Ancient Greeks:

There have been several periods in history when blonde hair has been popular or favoured. For the ancient Greeks, blonde was the hair colour of the gods. Saffron, henna and a variety of pastes from natural ingredients were used to achieve as light a tone as possible. Certain popular hair-tinting concoctions had some rather unusual ingredients, including lizard fat, swallow's droppings and the finely ground bones of bears.

The ancient Greek word, *xanthos*, suggests not only blondeness but also yellow, gold-yellow and touched by light. The writer Homer made not only the hero Achilles blond, but his horse too.

The Romans:

In ancient Rome, it was the tradition that ladies of the night had their hair lightened or wore blonde wigs to show their availability. This obviously gave an idea to Valeria Messalina, wife of the Emperor Claudius, who seems not to have been entirely satisfied by her husband's lovemaking. She had the habit of putting on a blonde wig, nipping out of the imperial palace and touting for trade on the streets. Word of her nighttime sorties got around among the randier ladies of town, and soon lots of them were joining her in their blonde disguises in search of carnal pleasures.

The Romans' fondness for blonde hair seems to have originated from their admiration of the locks of the slaves they had captured in Scandinavia and Northern Europe. They used a variety of hair-lightening potions, some more effective than others. One such potion was a mixture of rock alum, quicklime, elderberries, nutshells, wood ash and dregs of wine. In order to get the full reddish-gold effect it was recommended that the mixture was left on for several days.

The Renaissance –
Venetian Blondes:

During Renaissance times, ladies in the rich city state of Venice would wash their hair in rainwater and chamomile and then sit in direct sunlight with their long hair spread over the brim of very wide, crownless hats in order to lighten their coiffures. From contemporary records it would appear that the practice probably resulted in more sunburn and sunstroke than it did hair-lightening.

The Blonde in the
20th Century:

The 20th century's love affair with
blondes began in the Hollywood of
the 1930s with Jean Harlow, the
Platinum Bombshell, the first in a long
line which included stars of the 50s
and 60s like Doris Day,
Marilyn Monroe and Jayne Mansfield.

It seems rather ironic that at the same time as Hollywood was turning blondes into the American dream, the Nazis in Germany were also extolling the purity of the blonde as the Aryan ideal. The *Lebensborn* programme in the 1930s was set up so that 'Nordic-minded' children could be bred from selected parents because the Nazis believed that blonde hair and pale colouring denoted racial superiority.

There is a remote village in Paraguay called Nueva Germania, whose inhabitants are mostly blonde-haired and blue-eyed. The village's existence stems from the actions of the sister of the philosopher, Friedrich Nietzsche, who had the idea of breeding a master race in the depths of South America. In the 1880s she carefully selected a large group of people in Saxony, shipped them off to Paraguay and expected that, over a generation or two, a new super-race would result. Things turned out rather differently. Today most of the group's descendants are poor, inbred and diseased.

The 21st Century . . .
Dye Dye Baby

For those who are sickened by them, take heart: natural blondes are a dying race. Social integration has meant that light genes are being dominated by darker ones and soon mousy will be the lightest shade around – a problem that will be extensively highlighted, no doubt.

'In the primordial soup of genes caused by world migration and intermarriage the blonde will ultimately be superseded by dark-haired and dark-skinned races.'

STEVE JONES, PROFESSOR OF GENETICS,
UNIVERSITY COLLEGE, LONDON

Male Blonding –
Do Gentlemen
Prefer Blondes?. . .

'This day my wife began to wear
light-coloured locks, quite white almost,
which although it made her look very
pretty, yet, not being natural vexes me,
that I will not have her wear them.'

SAMUEL PEPYS, 1664

'A chaste woman ought not to
dye her hair yellow.'

MENANDER, 310 BC

'Like so many substantial Americans,
he had married young and kept on
marrying, springing from blonde
to blonde like the chamois of the
Alps leaping from crag to crag.'

P.G. WODEHOUSE

'My brother's a slum missionary
Saving young virgins from sin:
He'll save you a blonde for a shilling
By God, how the money rolls in.'

ANON

'It was a blonde. A blonde to
make a bishop kick a hole in
a stained-glass window.'

RAYMOND CHANDLER,
Farewell, My Lovely

'A blonde girl wearing a man's
shirt but in all other visible
respects unmanly to the point of
outright effeminacy.'

KINGSLEY AMIS

'God is a gentleman.
He prefers blondes.'

JOE ORTON

'She was a blonde nearly young
American woman of such dynamism
that the tideless waves struggled
to get farther up the beach.'

ANTHONY CARSON

In Vladimir Nabokov's famous novel *Lolita* the sultry nymphette has chestnut-brown hair. When it came to making the film, director Stanley Kubrick insisted that Lolita had to be a blonde in order to capture better the character's quality of seductive innocence mixed with adolescent sensuality.

Do Women Prefer Blondes?. . .

'Small, short-sighted, blonde, barbed – she reminds me of a bright little hedgehog.'

EDWINA CURRIE ON TERESA GORMAN

'Once I put that wig on, I didn't say an intelligent thing for four months. My voice went up. I walked differently. I'd ask incredibly stupid questions.'

SIGOURNEY WEAVER ON THE BLONDE WIG SHE WORE FOR THE FILM *Galaxy Quest*

The Blonde Leading the Blonde . . .

'If you're blond, as I am, and you have blond lashes, you have to wear mascara, otherwise you're invisible on stage.'

MICHAEL CAINE

'I love the strength of white blonde. Some people talk about having disasters while dyeing their hair – in my opinion you can never have a blonde disaster . . . I am always trying the latest products – whatever is new goes on my hair.'

DONATELLA VERSACE

'I've never been a fluffy sort of woman . . .'

CAMERON DIAZ, ON TRAINING TO BECOME A NEW CHARLIE'S ANGEL

Do Blondes Prefer Gentlemen? . . .

'It is possible that blondes also
prefer gentlemen.'

MAMIE VAN DOREN

The subject of a recent debate at the Oxford
Union was 'This house believes that blondes
prefer gentlemen'. Asked why, the new
President of the Union explained, 'I wanted
to make the whole thing a lot more fun.
We have tried to make the debates more
accessible because a lot of students
criticized them for being over-intellectual.'
The President of the Union is a blonde.

Do Blondes Have More Fun?. . .

David Hockney once explained on TV how and why he decided to bleach his hair and become the blond he is today. It was in response to a television advertisement he saw late one evening in New York City. **'Blondes have more fun,'** it said. **'You've only one life, Live it as a blonde!'** He immediately jumped up, left the apartment, found an all-night hairdresser there and then and followed the advice of the advertiser, Lady Clairol.

A government study has shown that
blondes do have more fun – they just
don't remember who with.

Where 'Blonde' Comes From . . .

There has been some discussion about the true derivation of the word **blonde**.

Most agree that it probably comes from the late Latin word, **blundus**, meaning *yellow*.

Others (probably blondes) argue that it comes from another Latin word, **blandus**, meaning *charming*.

Some synonyms for the word 'blonde' which are favoured by blondes ...

snow-white
angelic
platinum
golden
creamy
lustrous
sun-kissed
lily-white
buttery
brilliant
pure

Some synonyms for the word 'blonde' which are favoured by brunettes . . .

discoloured
pallid
bleached
washed-out
colourless
chalky
ashen
cadaverous
etiolated
fake
tarty

Hitting the Bottle – A Word on Hydrogen Peroxide . . .

Hydrogen peroxide, the principal active ingredient in hair bleach, is a naturally occurring substance. It is produced by both animal and plant cells.

Hydrogen peroxide was discovered in 1818, though its use as hair bleach did not start until the Paris Exposition of 1867, when its hair-lightening qualities were promoted by E.H. Thiellay, a British pharmacist and perfumer, and Léon Hugo, a French hairdresser. Sadly for the Anglo-French duo, since dark hair was particularly fashionable at the time, it was quite a few years before their product achieved much success.

The name which Messrs Thiellay and Hugo gave their product, a 3-per-cent solution of hydrogen peroxide, was 'Eau de Fontaine de Jouvence d'Or' or water from the fountain of golden youth – rather more attractive-sounding than 'peroxide' or 'hair bleach'.

Apart from its use in the creation of blondes, hydrogen peroxide is also used as a disinfectant, in fuel for rocket-powered vehicles, and in mushroom growing.

Bleaches and Cream – Other Ways to Go Blonde . . .

The writer Pliny recorded that various blonde washes were employed by Roman ladies two thousand years ago. One particularly popular product was a hair-lightening soap made from goat fat and beechwood ash. It was called 'Mattaic balls'.

It's Worth It
to Colour . . .

Well it is to somebody –
In America alone sales of hair-colouring
products are thought to be
worth nearly £1 billion a year. Blonde
is by far the most popular colour.

To Bleach or Not to Bleach? . . .

Madonna's career only took off in a big way in 1982 when she dyed her hair blonde. It has been suggested that her earning power since then can be precisely correlated with her changes in hair colour.

Life's a Bleach . . .

'The heck with the natural look.
After all, you can't take credit for
what you're born with, only for what
you do yourself. Where would
Marilyn Monroe be if she'd clung to
the hair colour God gave her?
We'd have a movie called
Gentlemen Prefer Mousy Brown Hair.'

ADAIR LARA

In 1955 Marilyn Monroe moved to New York determined to change her image. She threw a press conference to reveal the new Monroe. When she finally arrived all those present were puzzled as to what it was that was new about her. Questioned about it, Marilyn exclaimed, 'But I have changed my hair.' When asked to describe the new colour, Marilyn replied in her famous little-girl's voice, 'Subdued platinum.'

Blonde Movies . . .

Blonde Bombshell, Blonde Crazy,
Blonde Fever, Blonde Fist,
The Blonde from Peking,
A Blonde in Love, Blonde Sinner,
Blonde Venus, Blondes for Danger,
Blondie, Blondie Johnson,
Blonde of the Follies,
Don't Bet on Blondes,
The Adventurous Blonde,
Blonde Inspiration, Platinum Blonde,
The Real Blonde,
Gentlemen Prefer Blondes.

All the Fun of the Fair...

There are very few blonde jokes where the butt of the joke is not the blonde. *Here is one example:*

Three blondes were given a wish by a good fairy.

The first wanted to be even blonder, and her wish was granted.

The second wanted bigger breasts and was turned into Pamela Anderson.

The third asked to be made more stupid. Her wish too was granted – she was turned into a man.

Not So Nice Blonde Jokes . . .

Husband: As a start I think you should learn to iron, then we could do without the ironing lady.

Blonde wife: Well, if you would learn to f**k me properly we could do without the gardener!

A blonde and a brunette were discussing their boyfriends:

Brunette:	Last night I had three orgasms in a row!
Blonde:	That's nothing; last night I had over a hundred.
Brunette:	My God! I had no idea he was that good.
Blonde:	(*looking shocked*) Oh, you mean with one guy?

A blonde walks into a doctor's office. She gets in the room with the doctor and says, 'Doctor, I hurt all over.'

The doctor is really confused and says, 'What do you mean, you hurt all over?'

The blonde says, 'I'll show you.' She then touches herself on her leg. 'OW! I hurt there.'

Then she touches her earlobe. 'OW! I hurt there, too!'

Then she touches her hair. 'OW! EVEN MY HAIR HURTS!'

So the doctor sits back and thinks on it for a moment. Then he says, 'Tell me, is blonde your natural hair colour?'

The blonde says, 'Yes, why?'

The doctor replies, 'Well, you've got a broken finger!'

A couple of blondes were driving through Louisiana when they came to a sign that told them they were almost at Natchitoches. They argued all the way there about how to pronounce the name of the town. Finally they stopped for lunch. After getting their food, one of the blondes said to the cashier, 'Can you settle an argument for us? Very slowly, tell us where we are.' The cashier leaned over the counter and said: 'Buuurrrrrr-Gerrrrrr Kiiiinnnnnggg.'

Two blondes walk into a bar – well you'd have thought one of them would have noticed it.

Brunette: How many sheep does it take to knit a sweater?

Blonde: I didn't know they could knit.

A policeman pulls up alongside
a speeding car on the motorway.
As he peers through the driver's window,
he is astounded to see that the
blonde behind the wheel is knitting.

He shouts, 'Pull over!'
'No,' the blonde yells back, 'Scarf!'

A brunette, a redhead and a blonde decide to visit the ladies' room and find an old woman sitting at the entrance who says to them, 'Be sure to check out the magic mirror. If you look into it and say something truthful you will be greatly rewarded. But if you say something false you will be sucked into the mirror for all eternity!' The three women stand before the mirror and the brunette says, 'I think I'm the most beautiful of us' and in an instant she is surrounded by money. The redhead steps up and says, 'I think I'm the most talented of us' and she suddenly finds the keys to a brand new Lexus in her hands. Then the blonde looks into the mirror and says, 'I think . . .' and is promptly sucked into the mirror.

Are Blondes Really D'ummm? . . .

A recent article in *The Times* observed that there seemed to very few blond (or blonde) winners of Nobel prizes, but that the reason for this could simply be that Nobel Laureates tend to be older men whose hair is grey or mostly absent or both.

'I'm not offended by all the dumb-blonde jokes because I know that I'm not dumb. I also know I'm not blonde.'

DOLLY PARTON

'The one and original lovable monster is lost amid all the hydraulic manipulations in what now emerges as the story of a dumb blonde who falls for a huge plastic finger.'

JUDITH CRIST, REVIEWING THE 1976 REMAKE OF *King Kong* IN THE *Saturday Review* (THE ACTRESS WAS JESSICA LANGE)

'He is the only genius with an IQ of 60.'

GORE VIDAL ON ANDY WARHOL

Blonde Terminology . . .

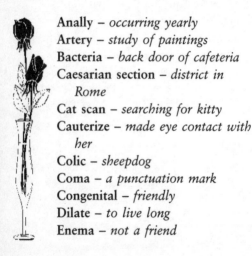

Anally – *occurring yearly*
Artery – *study of paintings*
Bacteria – *back door of cafeteria*
Caesarian section – *district in Rome*
Cat scan – *searching for kitty*
Cauterize – *made eye contact with her*
Colic – *sheepdog*
Coma – *a punctuation mark*
Congenital – *friendly*
Dilate – *to live long*
Enema – *not a friend*

Fester – *quicker*
Fibula – *a small lie*
Impotent – *distinguished, well known*
Intense pain – *torture in a teepee*
Labour pain – *getting hurt at work*
Medical staff – *doctor's cane*
Morbid – *higher offer*
Nitrate – *cheaper than day rate*
Outpatient – *person who has fainted*
Pathology – *a rambler's association*
Post operative – *letter carrier*
Protein – *favouring young people*
Radiologist – *Dr Fox on Capital FM*

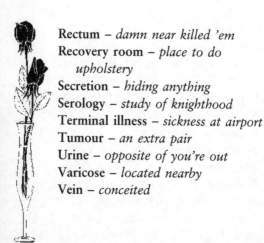

Rectum – *damn near killed 'em*

Recovery room – *place to do upholstery*

Secretion – *hiding anything*

Serology – *study of knighthood*

Terminal illness – *sickness at airport*

Tumour – *an extra pair*

Urine – *opposite of you're out*

Varicose – *located nearby*

Vein – *conceited*

Some Social Observations on Blondes . . .

What is the blonde's favourite battery?
Ever-Ready.

What is blonde, brunette, blonde,
brunette, ...?
A blonde doing cartwheels.

Why are blondes' coffins Y-shaped?
Because as soon as they are on their
backs, their legs open.

**Why do blondes get confused
in the ladies' room?**
They have to pull their own
pants down.

**What's a blonde's favourite
nursery rhyme?**
Humpme Dumpme.

Why do blondes wear pants?
To keep their ankles warm.

How do you know when a blonde's been in your fridge?
Lipstick on the cucumbers.

How do you tell when a blonde reaches orgasm?
1: She drops her nail-file.
2: She says, 'Next'.
3: The next person in the queue taps you on the shoulder.

Why did God create blondes?
Because sheep can't bring beer
from the fridge.

**Why do blondes drive cars
with sunroofs?**
More leg room.

Why do blondes have orgasms?
So they know when to stop having sex.

Why do blondes take the pill?
So they know what day of the week it is.

Why do blondes wear green lipstick?
Because red means stop.

Why do blondes wear hoop earrings?
They have to have somewhere to rest
their ankles.

Why don't blondes eat bananas?
They can't find the zip.

**What do blondes do after they
comb their hair?**
They pull up their pants.

What do you call a blonde lesbian?
A waste.

What do you call a blonde with a
bag of sugar on her head?
Sweet F. A.

What do a blonde and your computer
have in common?
You don't know how much either
of them mean to you until they
go down on you.

What do blondes say after sex?
Are you boys all in the same band?

**What is the connection between
a blonde and a halogen headlamp?**
They both get screwed on the
front of a Ford Escort.

**What do you call a blonde
with pigtails?**
A blow job with handlebars.

**What's the difference between a blonde
and an ironing board?**
It's difficult to open the legs on an
ironing board.

**What's the difference between a
blonde and a mosquito?**
When you smack the mosquito
it stops sucking.

**How does a blonde like her
eggs in the morning?**
Fertilized.

**What did the blonde's left leg
say to her right leg?**
Between the two of us, we can make
a lot of money.

What do a blonde and a turtle have in common?
If you get them on their backs they're both f**ked.

What is the difference between a blonde and an inflatable doll?
About 2 cans of hair spray.

What's the quickest way to get into a blonde's pants?
Pick them up off the floor.

**What does a blonde do if she is
not in bed by 10?**
She picks up her coat and goes home.

**How do you make a blonde
laugh on Saturday?**
Tell her a joke on Wednesday.

**How many blondes to make
chocolate chip cookies?**
25 – one to stir the mixture and
24 to peel the Smarties.

Why aren't blondes good cattle herders?
Because they can't even keep
two calves together!

Did you hear about the blonde who
tried to blow up her husband's car?
She burned her lips on the exhaust pipe.

How do you keep a blonde busy?
Write 'Please turn over' on both sides
of a piece of paper.

**What do you call it when a blonde
is taken over by a demon?**
Vacant possession.

How do blonde brain cells die?
Alone.

How do you brainwash a blonde?
Give her a douche and shake her upside
down.

What do you call a blonde
mother-in-law?
An airbag.

Why did the blonde stare at the carton
of frozen orange
juice for 2 hours?
Because it said 'concentrate'.

What's the difference between a
blonde and a computer?
You only have to punch information
into a computer once.

How can you tell when a fax has
been sent from a blonde?
There is a stamp on it.

What's the difference between a
prostitute, a nymphomaniac, and
a blonde?
The prostitute says,
'Aren't you done yet?'
The nympho says,
'Are you done already?'
The blonde says,
'I think I'll paint the ceiling beige.'

Why do blondes have 'TGIF'
on their shoes?
Toes go in first.

What do you call 15 blondes in a circle?
A dope ring.

What do you call a blonde
with 2 brain cells?
Pregnant.

What do you call a blonde in an
institution of higher learning?
A visitor.

What do you call a thought buzzing
inside a blonde's head?
A Space Invader.

What do you call it when a blonde
dyes her hair brown?
Artificial intelligence.

Final Word . . .

Things to do with this book:

For anyone who is not a blond/e:

a. File this book away in your toilet

b. Put it out for the dustmen – they are bound to like blondes

c. Throw it at a passing blonde and shout 'Fetch!'

For anyone who is blond/e:

a. Read it again because you heard it was good to recycle

b. Eat it because it's easier to digest that way

c. Regurgitate the contents if possible (preferably on a passing brunette)

Other 'Little Book' titles published by

Michael O'Mara Humour

The Little Book of Farting – ISBN 1-85479-445-0
The Little Book of Stupid Men – ISBN 1-85479-454-X
The Little Toilet Book – ISBN 1-85479-456-6
The Little Book of Venom – ISBN 1-85479-446-9
The Little Book of Pants – ISBN 1-85479-477-9
The Little Book of Pants 2 – ISBN 1-85479-557-0
The Little Book of Voodoo – ISBN 1-85479-560-0
The Little Book of Magical Love Spells – ISBN 1-85479-559-7
The Little Book of Bums – ISBN 1-85479-561-9
The Little Book of Revenge – ISBN 1-85479-562-7

*If you would like more information,
please contact our UK Sales Department:*
Fax: 020 7622 6956
E-mail: jokes@michaelomarabooks.com